Harriet Tubman
Leading Others to Liberty

Torrey Maloof

Consultants

Vanessa Ann Gunther, Ph.D.
Department of History
Chapman University

Nicholas Baker, Ed.D.
Supervisor of Curriculum and Instruction
Colonial School District, DE

Katie Blomquist, Ed.S.
Fairfax County Public Schools

Publishing Credits

Rachelle Cracchiolo, M.S.Ed., *Publisher*
Conni Medina, M.A.Ed., *Managing Editor*
Emily R. Smith, M.A.Ed., *Series Developer*
Diana Kenney, M.A.Ed., NBCT, *Content Director*
Courtney Patterson, *Senior Graphic Designer*
Lynette Ordoñez, *Editor*

Image Credits: Cover page Dayton Metro Library Map Collection; cover and p. 1 J. T. Vintage/Bridgeman Images; p. 2 Susan Pease Danita Delimont Photography/Newscom; p. 5 The Abraham Lincoln Papers at the Library of Congress; p. 4 (left), 6, 10, 16, 18 (bottom left), 20, 21 North Wind Picture Archives; p. 4 (right) World History Archive/Newscom; pp. 7, 8, 9, 11 Illustrations by Evan Ferrell; pp. 8, 18 (top right) 20 Granger, NYC; p. 9 Tarker/Bridgeman Images; p. 12 Bettmann/Getty Images; pp. 14-15 Bridgeman Images; p. 15 Public Domain; p. 17 MPI/Getty Images; p. 18 (bottom right) LOC [rbpe.33700200]; p. 19 National Geographic Creative/Alamy Stock Photo; p. 22 (left) Peter Newark Military Pictures/Bridgeman Images, (right) Congressional Quarterly/CQ Roll Call/Newscom; p. 23 NARA [299998]; p. 24 MPI/Getty Images; p. 25 (top) Randy Duchaine/Alamy Stock Photo, (middle) Susan B. Anthony Collection, Rare Book and Special Collections Division, Library of Congress (036.00.00), (bottom) New York Public Library, USA/Bridgeman Images; p. 26 Herb Quick/Alamy Stock Photo; p. 27 (top right) Vespasian/Alamy Stock Photo, (top left) LOC [LC-DIG-ppmsca-02909], (bottom) Creative Commons by Beyond My Ken, used under CC BY-SA 4.0; p. 28 Susan Pease Danita Delimont Photography/Newscom; p. 31 Sculpture by Jane DeDecker, photograph by Dwight Burdette/Wikimedia Commons; p. 32 New York Public Library, USA/Bridgeman Images; back cover page Susan B. Anthony Collection, Rare Book and Special Collections Division, Library of Congress (036.00.00); all other images from iStock and/or Shutterstock.

Library of Congress Cataloging-in-Publication Data

Names: Maloof, Torrey, author.
Title: Harriet Tubman : leading others to liberty / Torrey Maloof.
Description: Huntington Beach, CA : Teacher Created Materials, 2017. | Includes index.
Identifiers: LCCN 2016034147 (print) | LCCN 2016037576 (ebook) | ISBN 9781493838028 (pbk.) | ISBN 9781480757677 (eBook)
Subjects: LCSH: Tubman, Harriet, 1820?-1913--Juvenile literature. | Slaves--United States--Biography--Juvenile literature. | African American women--Biography--Juvenile literature. | Underground Railroad--Juvenile literature.
Classification: LCC E444.T82 M346 2017 (print) | LCC E444.T82 (ebook) | DDC 306.3/62092 [B] --dc23
LC record available at https://lccn.loc.gov/2016034147

Teacher Created Materials

5301 Oceanus Drive
Huntington Beach, CA 92649-1030
http://www.tcmpub.com

ISBN 978-1-4938-3802-8

Table of Contents

They Called Her Moses

I had reasoned this out in my mind, there was one of two things I had a right to, liberty or death; if I could not have one, I would have the other.

—Harriet Tubman

In the Bible, there is the story of Moses. Moses asked the Pharaoh of Egypt to set the enslaved Israelites free. The Pharaoh refused to free them. So, Moses led the Israelites out of Egypt to freedom. This was called the **Exodus**.

Like the biblical hero, Harriet Tubman led an exodus, too. After her own flight to freedom, Tubman made the daring decision to return to the South again and again. She made this journey to guide others to freedom. Tubman led more than 300 slaves to the North. Because of this, those who knew her called her Moses. This is just one remarkable story about Tubman. The truth is, her life is full of amazing stories!

Harriet Tubman

Moses leads the Israelites out of slavery in Egypt.

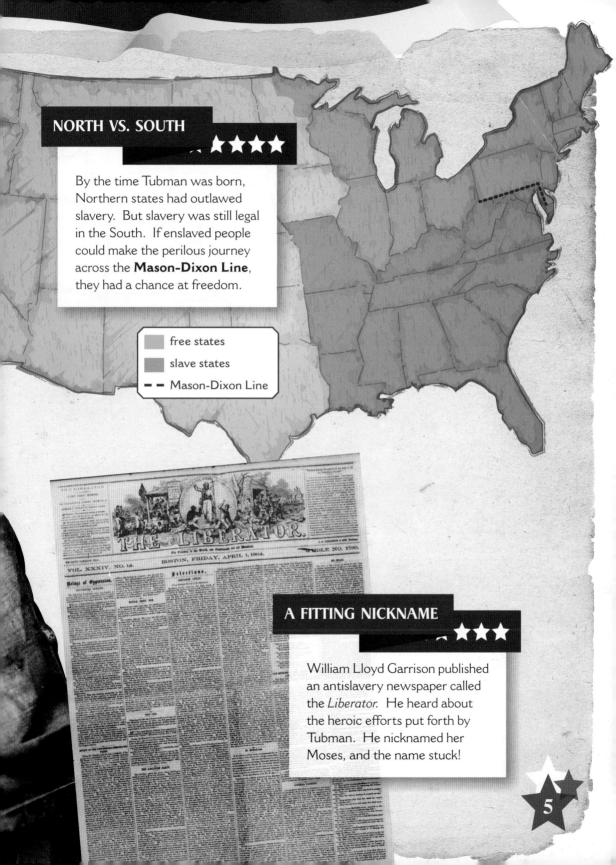

NORTH VS. SOUTH ★★★★

By the time Tubman was born, Northern states had outlawed slavery. But slavery was still legal in the South. If enslaved people could make the perilous journey across the **Mason-Dixon Line**, they had a chance at freedom.

free states
slave states
- - Mason-Dixon Line

A FITTING NICKNAME ★★★

William Lloyd Garrison published an antislavery newspaper called the *Liberator*. He heard about the heroic efforts put forth by Tubman. He nicknamed her Moses, and the name stuck!

5

Born into Slavery

No one recorded the date Harriet Tubman was born. This was common in the days of slavery. Very rarely were the birthdates of enslaved people recorded or remembered. They were not considered important enough for this.

Historians believe Tubman was born sometime between 1819 and 1822. Her birth name was Araminta Ross. Her parents called her "Minty." They were enslaved on a **plantation** in Maryland.

SLAVERY COMES TO THE UNITED STATES

Beginning in the 1600s, slave traders kidnapped Africans and brought them to the Americas as slaves. After being sold at auctions, enslaved people were forced to work by their owners. Enslaved people had no freedom and were routinely beaten.

an enslaved family on a plantation

Around the age of five, Tubman was hired out by her master, Edward Brodas. She had to leave her family and go to work for a nearby family named the Cooks. Life with the Cooks was hard for Tubman. They whipped her any time she made a mistake or made them angry. Tubman had many jobs at the Cook home. She cooked meals and cleaned. She helped Mrs. Cook weave fabric and wind yarn. Mr. Cook trapped **muskrats** and sold their valuable fur. He made Tubman watch the traps. Sometimes, when Mr. Cook was not looking, young Tubman released the muskrats from the traps. She wanted them to be free even though she could not be.

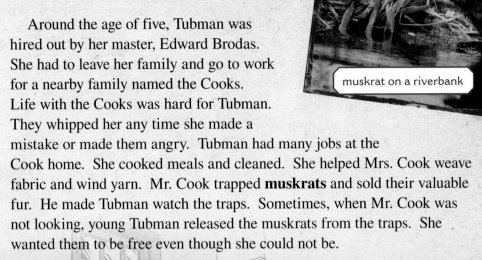

muskrat on a riverbank

Tubman works in the Cooks's kitchen.

Having to watch the muskrat traps meant that Tubman spent a lot of her time in freezing river water. She eventually caught a severe cold. Soon, the Cooks sent Tubman back to her master's plantation for being too weak and unskilled.

It was not long before Tubman's master hired her out again to another family. This time, her job was to look after a baby. If the baby cried during the night, Tubman was whipped. She was forever tired from staying up all night, every night, with the infant.

TRYING TO SURVIVE

★★★★★★★

Tubman learned tricks to help her endure slavery. She wore extra layers of clothes to protect her skin from the whip. She also screamed loudly during her beatings in the hope that they would be cut short.

One day while at the family's home, Tubman saw a bowl of sugar cubes on a table. She had never tasted sugar. Her curiosity got the best of her. She tasted one cube but was quickly caught. Tubman knew she was going to get whipped, so she ran away. After hiding in a pigpen for five days, she returned to her master's farm frightened, dirty, and hungry.

Tubman was not hired out again until she was older. Instead, she was sent to work in the fields. It was there that she heard stories about enslaved people escaping to freedom. She wondered if she could one day do the same.

enslaved people harvest cotton

A runaway slave is pursued by his master.

Even as a young teenager, Tubman helped others. One day, while working in the fields, a man tried to escape to freedom. He made a run for it! The **overseer**, whip in hand, saw him and gave chase. The man ran into a store to hide, but the overseer saw him. He instructed Tubman, who had run after them, to hold the man down to be whipped. Tubman refused. The man ran out the door. Tubman blocked the door, preventing the overseer from pursuing him. This proved to be a costly choice. The overseer picked up a two-pound weight and threw it at the fleeing man. But, he missed his target and hit Tubman instead. The weight struck her directly in the head. She instantly fell to the floor, unconscious. Her life would never be the same.

After the head trauma, Tubman suffered physically. She had unbearable headaches, **epileptic seizures**, and episodes of **narcolepsy**. But, she gained confidence. She had challenged the overseer. She stood up for herself and aided a person in need of help. As a result, her peers treated her with great respect.

Tubman lays unconscious after being struck in the head.

NEW NAME

★★★★★★★★

Tubman changed her name to Harriet, her mother's name, after being struck in the head. She wanted a more mature name. She changed her last name to Tubman in 1844 when she married John Tubman, a free black man.

11

Journey to Freedom

Tubman had long wondered if she was strong enough and smart enough to make the dangerous journey to freedom. Her father helped build up her confidence. He taught her valuable lessons. He showed her how to survive in the woods and on the run.

Tubman's father instructed her always to follow the North Star. If she could not see the star on a foggy or cloudy night, there was another trick. He said to feel the trees for moss, since the green plant grew on the north side of trees. Her father also taught her to hunt so she would have food. He showed her how to make a fire so she could cook meals and stay warm. Tubman learned how to swim, too.

Tubman always worried about being sold and sent further south. When she heard a rumor that her fears were about to come true, she decided it was time to go. She told her husband and two of her brothers her plan. In 1849, she and her brothers set out, but after a while her brothers grew fearful and wanted to turn back. After Tubman made sure they got home safely, she bravely set out on her own.

FEARS OF THE DEEP SOUTH

Many slaves were afraid of being sent to the Southeast United States, known as the Deep South. It was hot and humid there, and the work was hard. It was also farther away from freedom in the North.

enslaved people on a Southern plantation

Enslaved people escape under the cover of darkness, guided by the North Star.

moss growing on the north side of trees

13

Tubman began her harrowing journey under the cover of darkness in 1849. She worked her way through the woods of Maryland. She followed the Choptank River and used the North Star as her compass to freedom. Tubman waded through marshes and walked through creeks to help hide her scent from any hound dogs that may be looking for her.

Tubman received help from various people along the way. They housed her, fed her, and gave her clean clothes. And they instructed her where to go next and told her whom she could trust. This secret network of people and routes was the Underground Railroad. **Abolitionists** created it to help enslaved people escape to the North.

QUAKER HELP

★★★★

Quakers were the first religious group in the United States to ban slavery. Quakers helped enslaved people find freedom using the Underground Railroad. They worked hard to help end slavery.

a modern depiction of Harriet Tubman

While Tubman's exact route remains unknown, it is believed that she traveled nearly 90 miles to freedom. After a long and daring journey, she arrived in Philadelphia. She had crossed the Mason-Dixon line. She was free!

Tubman later reflected on this moment. She said, "When I found I had crossed that line, I looked at my hands to see if I was the same person. There was such a glory over everything; the sun came like gold through the trees, and over the fields, and I felt like I was in Heaven."

marker at the Mason-Dixon line border of Maryland and Pennsylvania

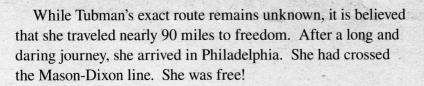

THREE HUNDRED DOLLARS REWARD.

RANAWAY from the subscriber on Monday the 17th ult., three negroes, named as follows: HARRY, aged about 19 years, has on one side of his neck a wen, just under the ear, he is of a dark chestnut color, about 5 feet 8 or 9 inches hight; BEN, aged about 25 years, is very quick to speak when spoken to, he is of a chestnut color, about six feet high; MINTY, aged about 27 years, is of a chestnut color, fine looking, and about 5 feet high. One hundred dollars reward will be given for each of the above named negroes, if taken out of the State, and $50 each if taken in the State. They must be lodged in Baltimore, Easton or Cambridge Jail, in Maryland.

ELIZA ANN BRODESS.
Near Bucktown, Dorchester county, Md.
Oct. 3d, 1849.

This 1849 document offers a reward for Tubman (Minty) and her brothers.

15

First Female Conductor

Tubman was free! As a free woman, she found a job in Philadelphia as a household servant. She loved that she was earning money for her hard work. She also loved that she had the right to quit her job if she so pleased. However, she was incredibly lonely. She had no one with whom to share this new life. Tubman missed her family dearly and worried about them. She decided it was time to go back and lead them to freedom, too.

Philadelphia in the 1840s

Harriet Tubman

Tubman was warned not to return to the South. It was too dangerous. She could be caught and forced back into slavery. But Tubman was determined. She saved her money and planned her trip south. With a lot of hard work and cunning skill, Tubman was able to bring her sister and her sister's two children to freedom in the North. Tubman had just become the first female **conductor** on the Underground Railroad!

Harriet Tubman with her family and other freed slaves

SECRET SLANG

★★★★★★★

It was of the utmost importance to keep the Underground Railroad a secret. To do this, people used code words. Below are just a few.

- "Lines" or "tracks" were escape routes.
- "Passengers," "freight," or "cargo" were people trying to escape slavery.
- "Stations" or "depots" were safe houses.
- "Station masters" were people who offered their homes as safe houses.
- "Stockholders" were people who helped fund the Underground Railroad.

After her first trip as a conductor, Tubman decided to do it again. In 1851, she returned to Maryland. This time, she wanted to guide her brother to freedom. Heading into the South was always dangerous, but now it was even more so. In 1850, Congress passed a new fugitive slave act. This law said that anyone caught helping people escape would be punished. Furthermore, it said that runaways who were caught in the North would be returned to their masters in the South. Or worse, they could be killed. But that did not stop Tubman! It inspired her to help free more people.

Soon, Tubman helped her brother reach freedom. Later, she helped her parents and other members of her family. But, she did not stop there. She made at least 19 trips to the South. She helped countless people escape. She never once lost someone, and she was never caught. A **bounty** was placed on Tubman totaling $40,000. That would be equal to over one million dollars today!

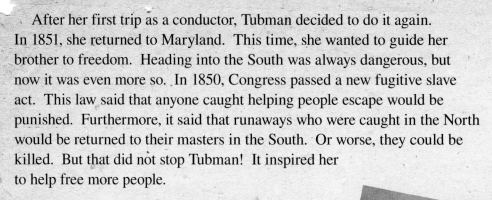

This 1851 document warns African Americans about slave catchers.

A slave catcher captures runaway slaves.

the Fugitive Slave Act of 1850

Harriet Tubman leads people to freedom in the Underground Railroad.

Union Army Member

Abolitionists wanted an immediate end to slavery. For more than 30 years, they had been working toward this goal. They held meetings and gave speeches. They sent out **petitions**. They wrote articles and circulated **pamphlets**. This was known as the Abolitionist Movement.

During this time, tensions between the North and South were rising. They argued over states' rights. They also disagreed on the economy, among other things. But all these issues had their roots in slavery. Northerners wanted it abolished. Southerners felt they had the right to retain it.

an ad for an abolitionist meeting in 1837

FREDERICK DOUGLASS ★★★★

One of the most celebrated abolitionists was Frederick Douglass. In 1838, he escaped slavery by heading to the North. He gave stirring speeches about his life as an enslaved man. He soon became the face of the movement.

Southern forces attack Fort Sumter.

Tensions reached their peak when Abraham Lincoln was elected president. The South feared that Lincoln would end slavery. As a result, it **seceded** from the **Union**. The Civil War began shortly after when the South attacked Fort Sumter.

Tubman quickly joined the war effort. She knew she could help. She became a member of the Union army. Tubman did many jobs for the army during the war. She was a nurse, a spy, a scout, and a leader.

Lincoln becomes the 16th president of the United States.

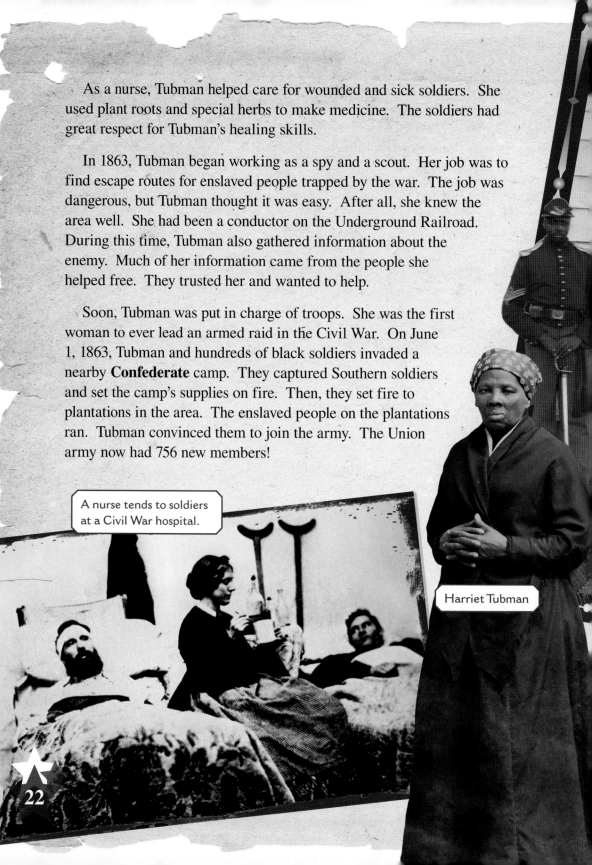

As a nurse, Tubman helped care for wounded and sick soldiers. She used plant roots and special herbs to make medicine. The soldiers had great respect for Tubman's healing skills.

In 1863, Tubman began working as a spy and a scout. Her job was to find escape routes for enslaved people trapped by the war. The job was dangerous, but Tubman thought it was easy. After all, she knew the area well. She had been a conductor on the Underground Railroad. During this time, Tubman also gathered information about the enemy. Much of her information came from the people she helped free. They trusted her and wanted to help.

Soon, Tubman was put in charge of troops. She was the first woman to ever lead an armed raid in the Civil War. On June 1, 1863, Tubman and hundreds of black soldiers invaded a nearby **Confederate** camp. They captured Southern soldiers and set the camp's supplies on fire. Then, they set fire to plantations in the area. The enslaved people on the plantations ran. Tubman convinced them to join the army. The Union army now had 756 new members!

A nurse tends to soldiers at a Civil War hospital.

Harriet Tubman

a company of black soldiers in 1864

EMANCIPATION PROCLAMATION

★★★★★★

President Lincoln issued the Emancipation Proclamation in 1863. It freed enslaved people in Confederate states and allowed black men to join Union forces. By the end of the war, about 200,000 black men had joined.

Caring for Others

Tubman stayed in the army until 1865. Then, she returned to her home in Auburn, New York. It was in this home that she helped take care of her elderly parents. Soon, she opened her home to others in need. She helped formerly enslaved people adjust to their new lives. She provided shelter for elderly, sick, and poor African Americans. But, she needed money to help care for all these people and for herself.

Gertie Davis

Nelson Davis

Harriet Tubman

MARRIED MOTHER

★★★★

Before the Civil War, Tubman returned to Maryland to bring her husband to the North. But, he had married another woman. After the war, Tubman met a veteran named Nelson Davis. The two married in 1869 and adopted a daughter, named Gertie.

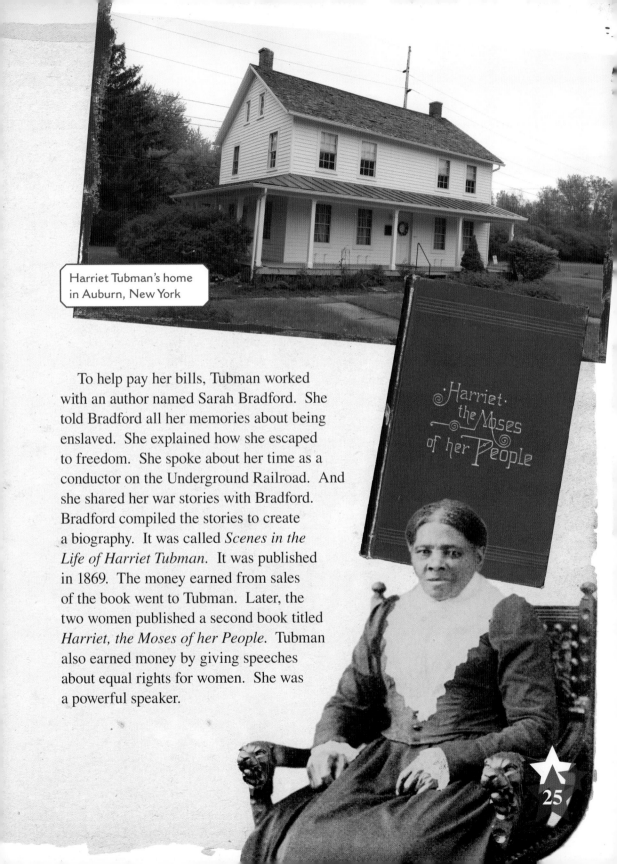

Harriet Tubman's home in Auburn, New York

To help pay her bills, Tubman worked with an author named Sarah Bradford. She told Bradford all her memories about being enslaved. She explained how she escaped to freedom. She spoke about her time as a conductor on the Underground Railroad. And she shared her war stories with Bradford. Bradford compiled the stories to create a biography. It was called *Scenes in the Life of Harriet Tubman*. It was published in 1869. The money earned from sales of the book went to Tubman. Later, the two women published a second book titled *Harriet, the Moses of her People*. Tubman also earned money by giving speeches about equal rights for women. She was a powerful speaker.

Rare Courage

Tubman continued to take care of others her whole life. In 1913, she became ill. She caught **pneumonia** (nuh-MOH-nyuh). Tubman died around the age of 93. She had lived a long and legendary life.

In Auburn, New York, people can visit Tubman's home. They can see where she helped those in need. The Cayuga County Courthouse has a **plaque** that talks about Tubman's "rare courage." It states how she "braved every danger and overcame every obstacle." The words are powerful and uplifting.

The National Park Service also honored Tubman. It set up a **monument** in Maryland. It includes 30 sites. They are each related to Tubman's amazing life. Some of the sites are in a wildlife refuge. This is where many enslaved people began their journeys toward freedom. Visitors can walk in their footsteps. It is a moving experience. And it is fitting tribute for a unique national hero such as Tubman.

HARRIET TUBMAN
1820-1913

THE "MOSES OF HER PEOPLE," HARRIET TUBMAN OF THE BUCKTOWN DISTRICT FOUND FREEDOM FOR HERSELF AND SOME THREE HUNDRED OTHER SLAVES WHOM SHE LED NORTH. IN THE CIVIL WAR SHE SERVED THE UNION ARMY AS A NURSE, SCOUT AND SPY.

MARYLAND CIVIL WAR CENTENNIAL COMMISSION

a marker at the birthplace of Harriet Tubman, part of the monument in Maryland

Harriet Tubman

IN MEMORY OF
HARRIET TUBMAN
BORN A SLAVE IN MARYLAND ABOUT 1821
DIED IN AUBURN N.Y. MARCH 10TH 1913

CALLED THE "MOSES" OF HER PEOPLE
DURING THE CIVIL WAR. WITH RARE
COURAGE SHE LED OVER THREE HUNDRED
NEGROES UP FROM SLAVERY TO FREEDOM
AND RENDERED INVALUABLE SERVICE
AS NURSE AND SPY

WITH IMPLICIT TRUST IN GOD
SHE BRAVED EVERY DANGER AND
OVERCAME EVERY OBSTACLE. WITHAL
SHE POSSESSED EXTRAORDINARY
FORESIGHT AND JUDGMENT SO THAT
SHE TRUTHFULLY SAID—

"ON MY UNDERGROUND RAILROAD
I NEBBER RUN MY TRAIN OFF DE TRACK
AND I NEBBER LOS' A PASSENGER"

THIS TABLET IS ERECTED
BY THE CITIZENS OF AUBURN
1914

CAYUGA COUNTY COURT HOUSE

Cayuga County Courthouse

Show It!

Harriet Tubman was born into slavery. Yet, she managed to escape to freedom and achieve many great things in her extraordinary life. Make a time line to show Harriet Tubman's life. Include key historical events that took place during her lifetime, such as the Civil War. Annotate the time line with pictures, quotes, or your own reflections about Tubman's life. Share your time line with your friends or family. Explain why Tubman was an amazing American woman.

Pennsylvania

Maryland

free states

slave states

- - Mason-Dixon Line

Glossary

abolitionists—people who were against slavery and worked to end it

bounty—an amount of money given as a reward for capturing a criminal

conductor—a guide, someone who helped escaped slaves get to the North

Confederate— the group of people who supported the South in the Civil War; comes from the name of the country formed by the states that seceded, the Confederate States of America

epileptic seizures—brief moments of convulsions or unconsciousness that are caused by a disorder of the nervous system

exodus—a mass departure of people from one place at the same time

Mason-Dixon Line—the dividing line between slave states in the South and free states in the North

monument—something that honors a special person or event

muskrats—a type of rodent that lives in or near water

narcolepsy—a medical condition in which a person falls asleep suddenly

overseer—someone who worked on a plantation and whose job was to discipline and control the slaves

pamphlets—small and short printed publications with no cover that is about a particular subject

petitions—written documents that people sign to formally request a change made by a superior

plantation—a large farm in the South that produces crops for money

plaque—a piece of metal or wood inscribed as a marker or memorial to mark an historic event or achievement

pneumonia—a serious medical condition that affects the lungs and makes it hard to breathe

seceded—formally separated from a nation or state

Union—term used to describe the United States of America; also the name given to the Northern army during the Civil War

Index

Your Turn!

An Inspiration

Harriet Tubman dedicated herself to helping others. She risked her life time after time to free people from slavery. After joining the Union army, she helped wounded soldiers and boldly led them in a raid. Later, she opened her home to those in need. Write a letter to Tubman explaining what you think is inspiring about her life. Include details from the book and questions you would like to ask her. Share your letter with your friends.